A Crack in
the Pavement

A Crack in the Pavement

text by Ruth Rea Howell

photographs by Arline Strong

Atheneum   1970   New York

*To the children of the
Mary MacCleod Bethune School*

OFTEN when you go outdoors, you're in a hurry—to get to the store with your mother, or downtown with your father, or around the block for a game of marbles, or to the park with your friends. But other times, you're in no rush at all, and you can just watch things happening in the city. These are the times when you can meet the animals and birds and plants and insects that live on your street. Or if you go to the park, you can run

very fast when you first get to the grass, but then you can slow down and listen and look, and you will begin to know some of your neighbors who never talk. Some don't even walk. Some just squirm, and some just spin; but they are alive just like you, and the city is their home, too.

How can you know who these neighbors are? For one thing, some of them move. You can watch a bird or an animal move. Of course, flags and airplanes move, too, and they are not alive. The difference is that they cannot decide for themselves whether to fly or be still. A flag only flies when the wind blows it, and a plane cannot fly unless a pilot is at the controls. But look far above your roof. Pigeons can fly without en-

gines. They are their own pilots. They decide whether to flap their wings or keep them still for soaring. Bikes and cars don't move without a driver, but an old horse can move by himself. His driver only guides him.

It is harder to be sure a plant is alive. If you see some green leaves in a crack in the pavement, don't just hop over them. Stop and take a look. The leaves are green and soft. If you squeeze a leaf, some green juice will cover your fingers. This green helps the plant to live and grow. Each green leaf is like a quiet factory, which can change air and water and sunshine into food.

Plants move as they make food and grow, but you never see them move. Growing is a much slower kind of moving than other kinds. The way to find out how much a plant moves when it grows is to measure it. On a spring day you may see a box filled with earth and some little plants that someone has just put outside his window, then go back after three weeks and look again.

The bean vine may have climbed up to the top and over to the other side of the window.

The stem of a very young tree is as thin as a pencil and as green as a leaf. But as it grows, each year it gets taller and thicker, and in time it is covered with a thick coat called bark. The stem has turned into a tree trunk.

Each different kind of tree has its own special kind of bark. You can make bark pictures by holding a piece of paper against the trunk of a tree and rubbing with a black crayon.

You may find a tree growing on your street with bark like a giraffe's neck. In springtime look up among its leaves, and you will see tiny green balls dangling on long stems. By the end of summer the balls grow bigger and softer. They are the yellow-brown "itchy" ball seeds of a London Plane tree.

A tree with long leaf branches and many pointed leaflets grows all over the city. It is an ailanthus tree. These trees grow everywhere, even in the cracks between two steps. Large ailanthus trees are as high as a house. No one takes care of them, but the rain waters them and on good days the sun shines on them, and air moves all around them. In summer ailanthus leaves are so long you can turn them into crowns and Indian headdresses.

The seeds of an ailanthus tree, from which new trees can grow, hang down from the top of the tree in fall in thick brown bunches. Each seed has a cover like a thin papery kite.

The wind blows the ailanthus kites all over town. If you find an ailanthus seed, plant it in a pot of earth and keep it on your windowsill. Water it, and wait patiently for a month. Then one day a tiny green stem will poke through the earth. By the time your tree is two months old, three or four leafy branches will be growing on the stem.

If you find a little plant growing in a crack with leaves as jagged as the teeth of a wild animal and flowers as gold as the sun, it is a dandelion; and it smells like a dandelion and nothing else. You can dig it up very carefully and plant it in a pot with some earth. The part under the ground is a root, and it may be longer than the leafy part. Your dandelion will need some water and some sunshine every day. First a tight green bud will grow. The bud will turn into a yellow flower, and that flower will turn into a fuzzy ball full of tiny black specks. The specks are dandelion seeds. If you or

the wind blows the seeds, they may fall to the ground far away from the plant where they grew. If the earth where the seeds fall is damp, and there is plenty of sunshine, the seeds will grow into more dandelions; for dandelions are alive, and all living things can make more of themselves.

Dandelions and ailanthus trees and most city animals and birds do not belong to anyone. They are not pets like canaries or cats or puppies. And they are not enemies like rats.

Squirrels, and sparrows and pigeons and insects and worms live in cities because they find plenty to eat there. Birds like to eat grass and dandelion seeds and insects.

Sometimes squirrels find something growing in the park that tastes extra delicious—mushrooms. You may find them, too. But remember you are not a squirrel, so don't eat them. Mushrooms grow very quickly in spring and summer, but they are not green like other plants. They are soft and round and brown like small umbrellas. They cannot make their own food from sunlight and air and water. They get all their food from the earth where they grow.

Squirrels also like to eat little bits of popcorn and pizza and peanuts that people drop when they go to the park. Pigeons and sparrows like them, too.

Some people take bread to the park for the birds and squirrels, and they let pigeons sit on their arms and shoulders as they feed them. But it is wiser not to touch a bird or animal you don't know.

Country birds build their nests in trees, and sometimes city birds do, too. But there are more windowsills than trees in a city, so sparrows and pigeons use them instead. They make nests out of twigs and grass and candy wrappers and kite strings and balloon strings and hair from long-haired dogs and hair ribbons from a girl who has lost hers. They use anything they can carry in their beaks.

After the mother and father pigeon build a nest, the mother lays two eggs. Then she takes turns with the father sitting on the eggs to keep them warm. After about two weeks a baby bird will peck its way out of each egg. A pair of pigeons may have two babies in the fall and two more in the beginning of spring and two more late in spring and two more in the beginning of summer and two more at the end of summer, which is why there are so many thousands of pigeons in a city.

Everyone tries to keep cool in hot weather. Birds do, too. But sparrows and pigeons like to take a kind of bath that you wouldn't like at all. If you find a little hollow place no bigger than your hand in the dust under a tree or a bush, it is a sign that a sparrow has made himself a dust bathtub. He flutters his wings and scratches with his feet in the dry earth until he has made a hole where he fits perfectly. Then he scatters the dust in between his hundreds of feathers. Soon he hops out of his hole and shakes all the dust out again.

Some city birds and insects are much harder to see than pigeons and sparrows. You have to listen for sounds and look for signs to find them. If you hear singing in the park or find a red-brown feather under a tree, look up. You may see a robin with his red breast. Robins eat insects and worms that live under the earth.

Earthworms make tunnels under the ground by eating up the earth ahead of them. When they go above ground, they leave tiny piles of waste earth called castings in the grass. After a hard rain in early spring, earthworms often crawl above the ground to breathe some fresh air, because the rain has pushed all the air out of their tunnels. You may find one wriggling on the sidewalk. Keep some earthworms in a clear plastic box filled with damp earth and watch them move. If you tried to move like an earthworm, you'd be very slow, and you would never be able to dig a tunnel without using your hands.

When you go to the park in the spring, look for tree leaves with holes in them. Ragged leaves are a sign that an inchworm is nearby. You may find a green inchworm chewing away underneath a leaf where it is hard for a bird to discover him. Or you may find one hanging in mid-air, because inchworms move from one part of a

tree to another by spinning an almost invisible silken rope and dropping slowly down from one leaf to another. Inchworms never bite and they have no wings, so it is easy to catch one and watch him move in your hand. Then put him back on a leaf and let him finish his green leaf dinner.

If you find a small sandy mountain in a crack in a sidewalk, it is a sign that ants are at work. You may see lots of very small brown ants hurrying in and out of the hole on top of the sand house they are building. Ants are insects. They have six legs and two strong mandibles attached to their heads. They use their mandibles for holding and chewing, and they can eat other insects much larger than they are. Many many ants live crowded together in each ant hill, and they are all brothers and sisters. They are as strong as moving men, so watch carefully and you will see them carrying their heavy loads of insects for dinner and sand grains for building their hill houses.

A soft white net in a window corner is a spider's home. If a fly or any other insect isn't careful, he may fly into a spider's web house and be caught there, and then the spider will eat him. A spider cannot fly to catch insects as a sparrow does. So he spins a web to catch himself a bug breakfast. Flies cannot escape from a spider's web because they cannot walk on the sticky silken strands; but the spider's eight feet never stick to his own web at all.

If you find some very small white shapes moving slowly along the branch of a bush, they are aphids, insects with woolly white coats. Woolly aphids make tiny holes with their mouths in plant stems. They suck out the green juice there for food. But a shiny brown ladybug with a black head and black dots on its back may be waiting on a branch of the very same bush to eat the aphids.

At the end of summer, some insects cover themselves with a tough gray or brown papery cover. Inside they will wait all winter long without moving or eating until spring comes again. Look for these waiting places called cocoons, tucked in the cracks of a wall or the bark of a tree or under the decorations of a stop light.

There are not so many signs to show the way to your neighbors when you explore in winter as there are in summer and spring, but on snowy days you can discover who has passed by, "reading tracks" just as the Indians used to do long before there were any houses at all in your city. Children make their own special tracks

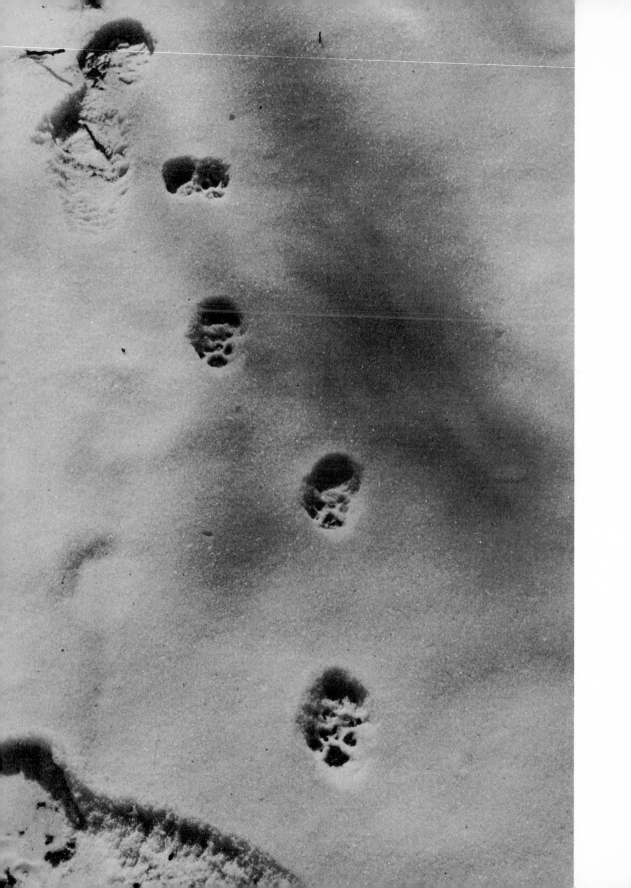

in the snow. So do cars and trucks. If you find a print with one big toe and four little ones, it is a sign that a dog or a cat has gone by, and you can tell the direction he was going, because the big toe is at the back and the little ones are in front. Four sharp toe prints mean a bird has hopped over the snow.

Cities are for people who play and work and go to school, but cities are for plants and birds and animals, too. If you keep searching wherever you go, you will discover more and more about all that's growing in your town the whole year through.